Faith to Finish

In the 11th Hour: Re-Discovering Your Purpose to Fulfill Your Destiny

Faith to Finish

In the 11th Hour: Re-Discovering Your Purpose to Fulfill Your Destiny

Dr. Michelle D. Bell

Pinnacle Point Publishing, Arlington, Texas

© by Michelle D. Bell

Published by Pinnacle Point Publishing

Printed in the United States of America

All rights reserved. No part of this publication may be reproduced, stored in a retrieval system, or transmitted to any form or by any means – for example, electronic, photocopy, or recording – without the author's prior written permission. The only exception is brief quotations in printed reviews.

Scripture quotations labeled (KJ) are from the King James Version of the Bible.

Scripture quotations labeled AMP are from the Amplified ® Bible (AMP), copyrighted © 2015 by Lockman Foundation. Used by permission. www.Lockman.org

Cover by Author

Dedication

I dedicate this book to My Lord, Jesus Christ, and the countless prophetic words over the years that helped me to stay in sync with God's plan for my life and family. I may have started out strong, stopped, and started again, but finishing is the ultimate goal and the joy it brings when completion is at hand.

I am thankful for all my children, grandchildren and my two great grandsons' for putting up with me. I know sometimes it seemed tough because I had a lot on my plate but know this was all for you!

And lastly, I want to thank my Aunt Doll Jackson-Davis who never wavered during the journey and supported me every step of the way. I won't stop asking the questions but can't promise I won't stop saying "I know"!

Table of Contents

Introduction	**11**
Chapter 1 – Changing from Resolution To Be Resolute	12
Chapter 2 – The 11th Hour	14
Chapter 3 – No Fear, No Doubt, Just Leap	18
Chapter 4 – Go Build, And God will Provide	21
Chapter 5 – Fortify Your Gates	26
Chapter 6 – Money Answereth All Things	30
Chapter 7 – Let's Pray Together	33
Chapter 8 - The Reproach Is Lifting, God's on Your Side	38
Chapter 9 - Shake It Off, And Let It Go, The Case Is Closed	41
In Closing	47
About the Author	50

Introduction

God had been worrying me about this word for some months, and I didn't know how to release it, so I was preaching to myself happy until I could do something with it. That's how it is sometimes. The title of my message is called, *Faith to Finish*. You can call it *Faith to Finish 20XX*. You can call it *Faith to Finish what God had me start that I stopped*. You can call it *Faith to Finish what I need to do for my life to change*. I purposely didn't finish the sentence because that will be personal to you. Faith to finish what? What do you need to finish?

Counting from November 11 each year is 52 days until the new year begins. Instead of holding to the tradition of resolutions that don't work, how about spending 52 days with God so He can help you re-discover your purpose? I have followed this process for many years and have seen God do the miraculous in my life. One of the things that pops out to me every year was God's infinite wisdom and sovereignty when He created special times to dwell with Him. Join me in the race to finish what you started so God can get the Glory and advance His Kingdom!

Chapter 1

Changing from Resolution to be Resolute

I'm a very numerical person. I'm in accounting and finance, but I'm very numerically inclined from a spiritual perspective as well, and God has graced me with my gifts of interpretation of time and numbers. One of the numbers that intrigues me very much is the number 11. This number means transition. When you count the days on our calendar from November 11th to December 31st, it's exactly 52 days. Many years ago, God began to deal with me about this whole new year's resolution, how people make resolutions on January 1st, and how they don't keep them. That's not how this process is supposed to work. When you follow the Hebraic calendar, the new year is around September, called Rosh Hashana. He began to deal with me about preparing before I got to the new year.

So, from November 11th to December 31st is 52 days. What impressed my heart during these years was preparing myself for January 1st. Not to wait until January 1st to come up with resolutions that I probably wouldn't even get through because God's plan is God's. It's not a coincidence if you're following the Hebrew calendar that the new year is before January 1st. Just think of it as getting to celebrate the new year twice!

The 52 days is the remainder of the year, when I seek the Lord, pray, and prepare communion. I am very involved in taking communion and understand the purpose for the believer, and I don't have to come to church to do communion. How can you do communion at home? There have been times when I didn't even have grape juice or a holy cracker, and I had to use a saltine and some water, and God still blessed me because it's about the act of obedience and the covenant that God has with us. For those 52 days, you begin to seek the Lord in your activities and what you will do for the following year.

How will it look from His mind, not yours, so that you're seeking the Lord for His guidance and plans for your life? One reason to do this is so that you can be on time. One of the things about time quite often is if you're not in the space and place that you need to be, someone else will miss their blessing. We hold up the blessings of others when we are not on time. When we push things off, we can miss it, and the opportunity may turn around and come back, and it may not. It might look like something else, but we can't continue to do what God has asked us to do.

Chapter 2

The 11th Hour

November 11th in any year is Veterans Day, and I thought that it was odd that God would bring that date to my attention, and I was curious about that because I wasn't quite sure I understood the 52 days or that I didn't understand the number 11. He showed me that the number 11 is for transition taking place, so whenever you see the number 11, there's some transition, and it could be good, or it could not be good because there's always an opposite in everything. Veterans Day is observed on that day, commemorating the end of WWI. Today we use it to honor military veterans. It was 11/11/1918 and the end of the war, but on 6/28/1919, the Treaty of Versailles was signed to end the battle completely. When you're talking about a treaty, you're talking about a truce, so at that time, that day was not called Veterans Day; it was called Armistice Day because that was the day that they put the truce into effect by the allies in Germany.

I'm giving you the backdrop because I want you to understand where I'm going with this from a spiritual and natural perspective. The signing occurred on the 11th hour, on the 11th day, and in the 11th month. If they couldn't get this truce signed, people would still fight with no resolution in sight. They had to sign this truce to end the war, transition to peace and freedom, and go home. There's also some significance in that God knew exactly what would happen that day. It is also interesting that's where we get the 11th hour from. When we're talking about the 11th hour in God's Word, Matthew 20:6-8 which talks about the parable of the vineyard workers not getting paid more than the workers that came at the 11th hour to work, during those times, the Roman workday was from 0600 sunrise to 1800 which would be 11 hours. So, it gives you more context regarding the 11th hour and where it comes from.

As previously said, there are 52 days to the end of the year from November 11, and this time can be used to seek God for the plan that He has for you for the following year. There are other connotations with the number 11, and it can either be positively related to transition or associated with mighty deeds and extraordinary acts of faith. When you look at Hebrews 11, it's the faith chapter, and why would God have Paul create a whole chapter on faith? Because he commemorated all the deeds, these people performed by faith in that chapter. He was honoring them by the acts that they had done because without faith, it's impossible to please God, and so you must have faith. Holy Spirit is coming back and forth on the Earth looking for faithful ones who are not looking to sway away from the

Word of Truth. We read in the word about the children of Israel; they really could not help themselves to keep the covenant. They tried and tried and tried, but something always happened, and of course, the negative connotation of the number 11 is disorder or chaos. How many of you have gone through something chaotic, but you have come out on the other side to transition with faith? Not only is Veterans Day commemorated in November, but it's also when our country took prayer out of the government and public schools on 11/22/1963. And what's interesting about that is that 22 is a double number, meaning that God will judge things. We've seen it happen and live in this time today. Putting prayer back in schools still has not been overturned. Then, of course, we all know about September 11, 2001, the towers in New York, and what this country has suffered because of the enemy that attacked us. God is our avenger; He will take vengeance on that situation. Lastly, there are many more events, but one you may not know or remember. I didn't want to bore you with the whole list, but many other things happened in the month of September. On September 22, 1963, President John F. Kennedy was assassinated, a president who most felt would do great things to help the people. He was going to sign laws, allowing people to see change. Then we all know that shortly after that, Dr. Martin Luther King, Jr. was assassinated, and many other men and women fighting for a better start so people could finish strong.

Chapter 3

No Fear, No Doubt, Just Leap

So, the 11th is an important number for God. All numbers are from God, but this one pretty much stands out for me. It's a time to review your plans so that you'll know exactly what you need to do to start the year right when you get to January. You want to be behind. Creating a vision board is one way to see how you should move forward. It's an excellent process to understand what's in front of you and provides a vision and a memorial for what God's plan is for your life.

Another way is journaling; I am also doing a lot of writing during this time and doing a lot of things that will help me transition so that when I get to the new year, I'm not behind. You must know the plans that God has for you and the path He wants you to take to get there because there are numerous ways that we can go, but we need to go God's way. We can stay on the path, but here's the thing about that; sometimes, we operate in fear and don't want to move forward because we don't want to make a mistake again and disappoint God. We've done some things before that weren't right on point. Those mistakes didn't get us where we needed to go, so we got fearful. We don't move at all, and that's not good either. You'll have to stay on course, take a leap of faith, and understand that you're under the great grace of God, which is sufficient to keep you and hold you. Don't be afraid to make a mistake. You got to be able to stay on the timeline because the enemy's objective is to get you off track and take you away from the promises and the plans of God. You can't wait until the first of the year to figure it out. You got to know beforehand before you get there.

We know that Hebrews 11 is the faith chapter, as we discussed. Hebrews 11:1 *"Now faith is the substance of things hoped for and the evidence of things not seen.* Hebrews 11:6, "B*ut without faith,* ***it is*** *impossible to please **him** for he that cometh to God must believe that he is and that he is a rewarder of them that diligently seek him* ." During this time frame, you'll diligently seek Him to understand what you're supposed to do to connect to the right path.

Part of the process will remove some people who can't go with you. Honestly, it may be family members that can't go or friends, who can't go with you. They've been your friend for 20 and 30 years, but they are not moving forward, and every time you try to take ten steps forward, something happens to make you go five steps backward. At some point, you must realize there's something wrong with this picture, which could be for that person too. You could also be a hindrance to that person, so you always have to check yourself. We have to continue to self-reflect.

That's the problem with the world today. We don't do a lot of self-reflection because we are afraid to be accountable; we don't want to submit our shortcomings and failures to God. Submission is a bad word, and if you can't be submitted to God, you can't be submitted to anything, your marriage, your children, your occupation. It will not work out if you're not submitted to God. I'm sorry it's not going to work out because that's where the covenant takes place with you and God seated at the table amid your enemies; only God can do that; a man can't do that, only God.

Chapter 4

Go Build, and God Will Provide

To provide you with an understanding of those steps in the plan, we'll go over Nehemiah 6:15 because this scripture is the basis of this book. God began to talk to me about Nehemiah again this year, but He gave me a different perspective about Nehemiah and what he had to go through to get those gates built back because the city was torn down. The wall was finished on the 25th day of the month Elul in the Hebrew Calendar; within 52 days, they were able to accomplish a miraculous feat. They had so much opposition to rebuilding the temple and the walls for many years. Encompassing in those walls were 12 gates to get into the city. Most of you know when it comes to walls and gates, the enemy has a way to get in if those walls are not shored up on a foundation; if they are not tight and right, the enemy will come in. He will look for any crevice underneath, and any little spark of light, he will try to go in and make it dark for you. We know that, naturally, gates are places where things happen, commerce occurs, and governmental things take place at the gate. Then we got our physical body and all the gates we deal with: our eye, ear, and mouth gates. How are your gates?

Are your gates shored up? We'll have to look at it because if your gates are not shored up, you will let anything come in. It's getting to the point where you can't watch television or a commercial. As a matter of fact, you can't even let your children watch a cartoon. We need to make some biblical cartoons for children because they are creeping the world in any way they can. They've been doing it for years, and we have not been saying anything. We sat in the church, stayed quiet, and let it happen. We were off our game, and we let them come into our gates, and now you have to shut the television down. I'm ready to cancel cable, they charge me all this money, and I can't even watch any decent thing on it. With cable television prices, we should at least have suitable programming. We need to make sure that we're shoring up our gates. Sorry, let's get back to the story!

In that scripture, the wall was finished in the month of Elul within 52 days. The month of Elul happens between August and September, and it's right before the Hebraic new year. It's interesting because it is a time of self-reflection before they enter that new year called Rosh Hashanah. Interestingly, he would end up being there in Judah at that time. Ezra was the religious leader during this timeframe, and Nehemiah was the official governor of the Persian province of Judah. You can read that in

Nehemiah 5:14. I referenced that because we have the religious leader and the government leader, priest, and king working towards the same goal. Nehemiah wasn't the king, but he was a governor. He had power, but we're talking about the fact that we have priestly and kingly assignments in us, and so we have the ability from God, with Jesus being our chief intercessor in heaven, to be both. In the book of Ezra, it's explained that Judah was in a ruined state and the walls were torn down, and the people that were already living around Judah and Jerusalem were opposed to the rebuilding. So a letter-writing campaign began, and the enemy started telling lies about the Jewish people. They started saying, "they're a rebellious group; they are not going to serve the king as they should ."The king will not be able to get his taxes; he will not be able to get his money if the wall is built back up. Isn't it interesting how all the other provinces have their walls intact?

Nehemiah is saying, why can't we have walls protecting our city? Which caused Nehemiah to be perplexed about the condition of his people. He couldn't understand it, and one of the reasons why the wall needed to be built back up was because the enemy kept on infiltrating their city. They kept on stealing from them, stealing their cattle, taking their children, and taking their women. It got to the point they didn't have any money, so they ended up mortgaging off their property and their homes. Everything was gone, and everything was lost. The people were in a state of brokenness. They had to borrow money to pay the tax to the king. We have something familiar to that today; it's called debt. It was absolute torture.

Nehemiah returns to Judah thirteen years later, and the temple is done, but the walls are still not built up, and the people are still in distress. The enemy still bombards them because they need to repair the walls. So, he begins a campaign, and these 52 days are important because God performed a miraculous feat. There's no way this could have been done when you had 20 years to do so, and you couldn't get it done, but he gets it done in 52 days. He goes before the king, and the king says, "why are you so solemn today?" Nehemiah said, "well, if it pleases the king." Now, where have you heard that verse from? In the Book of Esther, she said, "if it pleases the king." Esther went before the king so that she could free her people from the plot of Haman because he wanted to kill all the Jewish race.

Nehemiah prayed for two months, went before the king, and said, "Well, this is what I need, the lumber to rebuild the wall. I need a letter for the governor across the river so that he doesn't stop me from passing through. I need a letter to give to the people that are harvesting the forest trees that you control so I can get the wood to rebuild". Then he said, "I need some money," and the king said,

"Okay, you have whatever you want. Go get it, and I'll write the letters for you, and you can take them with you". God's favor and authority in action.

Chapter 5

Fortify Your Gates

Well, the enemies down in Judah and Jerusalem found out about what was happening, and they were not happy that these walls were getting ready to get fortified again. They were unhappy because they remembered this interfered with their thievery and harassment of the people. I know most of the time when I preach, it's about money, but it's always about money. Everything is always about money. Everything that our government does it's about money. The Bible says money answereth all things; it doesn't mean that you make money your God. God knows that money is an answer for the troubles on this Earth, and He needs kingdom citizens to spearhead it. He needs kingdom citizens to be over the bank accounts. God needs kingdom citizens to give where He says give, Amen. You need to be qualified to get to do that, and so Nehemiah was qualified; he sought God, so the walls to be built are to protect the city and its residents. Whenever God gives an assignment, He always provides provision.

Gates have various meanings but during this time is where business and everyday life were conducted. Ultimately, the gates are needed for protection when the walls go back up. When you inspect your gates and see what's open, you need to determine what should be closed and how to do so. The enemy comes to kill, steal and destroy anything and everything you have connected to God, including yourself. You have to fortify your gates.

We discussed the human gates of the ear, nose, mouth, eyes, and touch. You can't talk to people in any way, especially without showing the love of Christ. You can't keep cussing, and you're a Christian. You can't just keep talking to your kids without love and respect. What used to work back when I was a kid doesn't work today. I had a fear of my mother. Her name was Elvira, and she did not play. We also feared God, but she was in the natural. She was a little lady, but she was heavy-handed. She had these skinny narrow fingers, but when she hit you, you felt it, and you didn't dare cross her. Let me move on; that hurt. You are going to have to do what's necessary to make a change in this area.

Let's say you're in a marriage and know things are happening, and you're not giving it your focus. I remember going through something, and God kept saying, "you need to be quiet. Until I say something, I need you to be quiet". I learned through that transition that you need to be responsible for yourself and let God take care of the rest. When I began to be quiet, Mr. Bell was okay. At the end of the day, he heard God too. I'm not his boss, and I'm not his mama. I was running the household; I thought I was back in the day. That's that submission thing again.

I had to back it up. Whenever I counsel women who are thinking about getting a divorce, leaving their husbands, or having problems, the first thing I ask them before I pray is, do you want to stay in your marriage? Because we are not going to pray against what you want to happen, so if you say you're not sure or don't want the marriage, we're not going to pray about that part. We will pray for clarity and understanding for your next steps. Sometimes, you must be quiet and let God be God. It's a tricky thing. Sometimes you must sit there and be quiet and hear Him. Sometimes we can't listen to him because we're too busy talking. You're sitting down in prayer, and God is trying to say something, but He can't say anything because you keep talking. Sometimes you have to be quiet. There's nothing wrong with meditation. Meditation is not the enemy. You are just sitting there and being quiet so that you can try to hear what God is saying.

God is designing a fortified city of walls around you so the enemy can no longer encroach on your pathway and destiny. It cannot hold you hostage anymore, so we're going to decree and declare today before you go and do another thing; we're declaring that we are free from all entanglements, bondage, and servitude of the enemy in Jesus' Name. Amen. We will no longer have an encroachment on our path and the plan God has for us. We talked about the spiritual gates and fortifying them, and now you know what to do from a natural and spiritual perspective.

Chapter 6

Money Answereth All Things

Back to Nehemiah and his building of the walls in Jerusalem. Many things were going on during this time, and not only did Nehemiah have to deal with the construction of the walls, but there were other problems as well because there was discord amongst the people. There were enemies among them. Then to top it off, his Hebrew brothers and sisters were intermingling with the other folk, which is one of God's commanded not to do. He said not to do that because when you start mingling with other people not of your faith, you slowly start moving to their side, and you start following their gods and customs. You start mixing it all together, and that's what the world is doing today. They're mixing it all so that the Christian dynamic is not pure. That's why we need to focus on the Kingdom of Jesus Christ because when we focus on the Kingdom and we can talk to people about the Kingdom, it gives them a new perspective on the Christian way. Nehemiah had everything financially to move the plan forward, but the people could only get on board once they changed their attitude.

When God anoints you to move on the path and plan He has for you; you must know He will provide everything you need. The problem is that it might be different from what you think. I've had a 501c3 since 2004 and have done many extraordinary community endeavors and blessed people. I was saying to God one day, "When will this thing take full effect? When is it going to take full force?" Recently I had that conversation, and God asked me, well, are you ready? I thought I was. You need to go back and review the plan because what was right in 2010 needs to be corrected for today.

My plan for you is more significant than you realize; you had it at a smaller level. You got to understand that this thing is much bigger than you. I had to test you first. I had to take you through the fire first. I had to know that I could trust you. I had to see that you were going to take care of my people like I would take care of them. I had to know that you would love my people as I love them. Being in finance is one thing, and you never have financial problems. You never had your lights turned off. You never had the car repossessed. You've always had more than enough money to buy food and everything. It's one thing to be a finance person, but you need to understand the financial troubles of the people. I had to go through some things so that He could trust me. I had to come out the other side of some things so that He would know that He could trust me with his millions because that's what this will be about.

This is going to be a continual supernatural wealth transfer that God is going to need to happen so that kingdom citizens can be the answer to the world's problems. We'll have to be the answer, and one of those prerequisites is you've got to tithe. You're taken off the list right off the bat because that's the first question we're going to ask. Are you tithing? That's a taboo subject, but we're going to talk about your pocket because if you're not tithing, you will not be considered. That will be a prerequisite for God because, again, not only is that a faith thing, but it's an obedience thing, a submission. If you can't do that, then you can't do everything else that follows along with that, especially from a financial perspective. God already knows so that He will prepare you with your finances. He already knows the opposition that you're going to have, so He's already prepared for it. He already knows the beginning from the end and will not give up the fight. Too many times, we give up the war and run and hide. We hide because of shame and because of the reproach.

Chapter 7

Let's Pray Together

Nehemiah was in Shushan at the time. At the beginning of this chapter, they were talking about shame and reproach, and he was concerned about the survivors that had gone back there still dealing with the enemy's oppression. He said in the scripture that they were greatly distressed. The wall of Jerusalem was also broken down, and its gates were burned with fire. The first thing he said was he prayed for direction. You must have a life of prayer. I remember when God told me I needed to pray for people. I said, "well you know you could leave that to the other people. I'm just going to go ahead and do the word. He said, "no, you need to pray." I'd be in meetings with my cousin, Belinda; she would be so loud praying. I would be sitting there embarrassed. I'd be sitting there praying to myself; then I don't know what happened.

One day the Holy Ghost got a hold of me, and it was all over. I was louder than she was because we couldn't sit there in praise and worship to be quiet. We got to be loud and bold and chase those demons out. We're going to have to be loud. I'm already loud by nature. It was interesting when it came to prayer; I was loud because all the women in my family were very loud, except my great grandmother, quietest lady you ever want to meet. When my husband married me, he said we had to buy a house with two living rooms. One living room was his, and one living room was ours. He braced himself every time we hosted Thanksgiving or Christmas. Here they come! He used to talk so softly, and then he would get mad if you asked him what he said. If you asked him what he said more than twice, he wouldn't tell you anymore. If you didn't get it, you lost it.

I remember one time we were at my auntie's house. I flew into Rhode Island, and my brother and cousin came over. There are six of us; there are four girls and two boys. The boys were sitting there, all the girls and then the girlfriends. We were in the kitchen with my aunt. My aunt turns around and says to my brother, "how come you're not giving your opinion?" He said they wouldn't let us talk, so whatever they decide, we will do. I had no idea that all our life, that's what it was. The boys just followed us. It was the weirdest thing. I had no clue, but they figured out who the boss was. That wasn't it; it was just because we were the loudest in those situations. We wanted to be heard, and we were.

Anyway, let's get back to Nehemiah and prayer. In chapter two, he talks about distress, and he loves the city of Judah, and he's so upset about the problem he asks explicitly what he wants. While praying for these 52 days, ask God for the details. He's given me so many details I had to put the pen down. I'm telling you, He's a detail-oriented God. He will provide you with all the necessary elements. What gets us hung up is when He begins to give us the details, and we are too busy trying to figure out when, but that's not our issue. We must do what He asked, and then He'll reveal the time. That's why when we give a word of knowledge and prophecy and pray for people, I'm cautious about telling people a time frame. Because when that time frame doesn't come along, oh boy! I will say what thus sayeth the Lord, and it will be between you and Him.

It's in God's time, not my time, because we don't know the day, time, or hour. So, you're going to write the plan. Nehemiah wrote the plan God gave him in prayer, asked for written letters to governors, and then asked for the letters for the keepers in the forest. Everything seems to be going well until the enemy hears about it. In Nehemiah 2 and 10, Sam Ballet, Horn the Horonite, and Tobiah the Ammonite, the official, hear of it, and they're deeply disturbed that a man had come to see the well-being of the children of Israel. This is what happens when you arrive on the scene; the enemy gets mad. The other day, I heard a word from God that He was raising up the whistleblowers. I can't tell you why that was significant for me, but God was saying, how long are you going to sit there and let this stuff happen to my people? The other thing, too, is if you don't start speaking up, you will end up staying there longer than you have to because it could be that you're supposed to speak up about a thing. You're not going to be released from it. You're wondering when God will let you out of that thing, but He isn't going to let you out of it until you do what he said and move on to the next thing. When can I get out of here? Is it time yet? I'm tired of this job, but did you do what I asked you to do? Did you pray for what I told you to pray? Did you do this? Did you do that? They went to the king, and they lied to him about Nehemiah. The king had a lapse of judgment, so he had to go back and deal with that. When you start discussing your plans, adversaries will begin working against you. You must be careful who you talk around. They hate the favor you have in your life, and they will no longer have access to steal your plans, ideas, and dreams. That's what the enemy has sent them to do.

Present Day: The girlfriend of yours that's not married, but you are, and you keep hanging around her, and all she's trying to do is break you up from your husband, and vice versa. She thinks she knows everything about you, bringing up all kinds of false accusations. We need to be careful. They'll tell lies, they will agitate, and they will cause all sorts of confusion. You will have to stand firm and see the salvation and protection of the Lord to see your plan through, to see your pathway. Though the path might have some rubble on it, some tree limbs might have fallen, and there might be all kinds of obstructions, but they can be moved out of the way. You need to trust God. Nehemiah 4:4 said, "H*ear O our God for we are despised and turned their reproach upon their own head and give them for a prey in the land of captivity:*" because Nehemiah was getting upset, he said, "*And cover not their iniquity and let not their sin be blotted out from before thee: for they have provoked thee to anger before the builders.*" He said I'm sick of this reproach; I'm sick of the lying on me. How many of you are sick of people lying to you and about you? He was sick of it, and in verse 6, he said, "so built the wall and all the wall was joined together unto the half thereof for the people had a mind to work," let's be mindful.

Chapter 8

The Reproach Is Lifting, God's on Your Side

I will talk about distress and reproach because it just blessed my spirit. I knew I was having a problem and needed help understanding what the problem was and what to do, what God revealed to me as I had some shame that I needed to deal with, and it had to do with the financial realm. I couldn't figure it out because I said well, God, I repented for not being a good steward, so I don't understand what this is about. So shame comes along, and it makes you think you're not worthy, it makes you think that you can't do the plans for God, and distress means that it's terrible trouble, evil afflicted and shame is wicked. It's wicked, it causes injury, and it tries to break your spirit, and that's precisely what was happening to me; my spirit was damaged in a particular area, and I didn't realize it.

Let's go to Psalm 69: 5-7. I'm not going to be long; I am wrapping up. *"God, thou knowest my foolishness, and my sins are not hidden from thee. Let not them that wait on thee, oh Lord God of hosts, be ashamed for my sake: let not those that seek thee be confounded for my sake, O God of Israel. Because for thy sake, I have borne reproach; shame has covered my face.* S*hame* is disgrace, you're confused, you feel dishonest, and you're insulted". You are clothed with shame.

Do you remember the story about Adam and Eve? So, I don't have to go there, but you know they felt shame because they ate the fruit of the tree. They realized they were naked. Naked refers to shame. Shame is something that you put on yourself because you don't believe that God forgives you. You don't think that Jesus died on the cross and rose again for you. You don't believe that his blood can cover it even after you repent, so the devil will keep you in that shame. You hide yourself from others; you don't share that testimony because it's too painful.

You're walking in that shame, and today we are going to be free from the shame! But then we get to the reproach. Let me tell you this, to be made ashamed can happen through disappointed hope. You were hoping something would happen, and it didn't happen the way you thought because the enemy came in, and now you have shame to pierce or prick you. However, we are covered by the blood of Jesus, and our repentance and His forgiveness blot out our sins. I got a revelation this morning on why the enemy does not want the church to have the idea of repentance because he wants to keep us in shame. He doesn't want us to have the victorious life the Bible says we can have. The world and the church are minimizing repentance, just letting everything go.

We're not calling people to the carpet, we're not making people accountable, and we wonder why the spirit of the living God doesn't want to dwell there because there's no spirit of repentance.

It is a lifestyle; if I have to repent a hundred times a day, I hope not, but if I have to repent a hundred times a day, I will because I have to be right with God. It doesn't matter what man thinks anymore in my life. I'm telling you now I don't have to live with it, and we're going to talk about reproach, disgraced, scorned, contempt, despised, slander, you're blasphemed, and it's all resting on the condition of shame. Reproach is not something you've done; it is something that somebody else does because they think they know your business and believe they can bring it up at any time, even though you're a new creature in Christ, even though you repented to God, your children, your spouse, your parents, or your best friend. Whoever thinks they know your past is where this reproach comes in because they don't want to let it go. You hear you were that way before and will always be that way. So reproach sits on top of shame, and it's not enough that you already feel bad yourself, but now other people are putting stuff on you too. I say not today.

Chapter 9

Shake It Off, And Let It Go, The Case Is Closed

When God started talking to me several months ago about removing the reproach from me, I was captivated by the idea of totally being free, and then he kept saying it. For me, when He keeps saying something, then I must be missing what He is trying to tell me. Then one day, I started to think about what He was talking about, and he began to reveal that stigmatism to me.

The stigmatism you can't see because you may not have changed. Don't mean I didn't change; doesn't mean I haven't changed. We might have accepted Christ simultaneously, but I'm not you; I'm trying to live a life of holiness. I'm trying to live a life of righteousness. I'm trying to be truthful. I'm trying not to tell a white lie. I'm trying to love my brother and sister the way Christ loves them. I'm trying to come to church every Sunday even though I know that person hurt me and lied and said it was me and not them, and that's why they're leaving the church by groves. The offense is an entirely different message, but we must get over it because offense stops us from reaching our destiny, controls us, takes us off the yellow brick road, destroys us, and ruins relationships; the offense has to be cut out.

So, reproach is important. Remember what I said you're covered with reproach by others who know of or think they know about your condition and will run it into the ground. But God said shame and reproach are a foothold or a placeholder in your timeline that the blood of Jesus can remove at the root of your repentance. So repentance is going to be necessary. He forgives, and it doesn't matter what anybody else says. Shame says I hate myself for what I did, and God says I love you despite what you did. My God loves me, and He loves you, and I will not carry that baggage anymore. I'm walking in a new place and design and now understand He's been dealing with us for years and years. This is not something that just came up because if He had to deal with every solitary thing we did in our lives; we probably would be broken, so he takes time to deal with things.

There's a time factor to things He needs to handle in us, but I had to go to the courts of heaven and argue my case. I had to say this because mitigating circumstances required to be heard. All the evidence was not, and I needed to speak my case. I have a more favorable cloud of witnesses that could testify of my innocence, the angels rejoicing for me, and Jesus sitting on the right hand of the Father. I was bamboozled, tricked, and because of my ignorance, I succumbed to the enemy's devices because that's the world we live in today. It doesn't make sense when we're talking about debt and this country. When our economy decided to devalue the dollar by no longer backing it with gold and started using credit, God's name was no longer on the money system. God is no longer remembered in your finances; that's what they wanted. The enemy wished for everything to be done the way it is today, which is not suitable for us. That is why, as Kingdom citizens, we must recognize the monetary system we support. We live outside of those realms and live in and support a different financial system.

I was fed lies by a system that was not for me. I was told I could live a life of debt and still prosper, but the enemy still tried to destroy my good name. I almost ruined my good reputation with my credit and financial decisions that I could never take back—all these things that we do as Christians, as kingdom citizens, living like the world. Maxing out our credit cards and living beyond our means that's not right; that's not God. It is not the best that He has for us as His children. There is a witness in heaven named Jesus, who became my chief intercessor. He was my attorney in the courtroom. He was my advocate, and He knows all about me. He knows every dirty deed I have done, and He's forgiven me; he's moved the reproach off of my life, finances, body, and good name but not because I'm worthy but because I cost something to Him. I am his most valuable and precious possession, and I heard the Judge say, this case is dismissed! The reproach has been moved; the encroachment can no longer occur, and your access is denied. Today, you will know that you are transitioning into a place of Goshen. You will see that you are transitioning to a place of prosperity; you will be healed, delivered, and set free in all manners. You're going to pray for direction. You're going to ask precisely what you need. You're going to ask God for forgiveness and repent. He's moving the reproach off of your life.

Keep the spiritual things of God, and don't defile your gates. Keep the tithe and the offerings; they belong to the priest. They belong to God, and then don't overextend yourselves financially. Things are going to turn around. God reminded me of what happened when I was a child. When drive-in theaters were the entertainment spot, they also had playgrounds for the kids with round merry-go-rounds, and I said, "God, why are you telling me this?" That was the worst day of my life. I think I was 12 or 13; my Godmother, her sister, and everybody wanted to go to the drive-in movie, and I was responsible for taking all the little kids to the playground. So the little kids decided they would move the ride around real fast, and my hands slipped, and I flew off the ride. They had to call an ambulance, which was the worst day of my life. I was so embarrassed, and I don't think they were mad, but they couldn't finish watching the movie.

But what he showed me was, Michelle, you're on that merry-go-round, and it's going so fast, it's going so fast, the enemy can't even touch you, the enemy can't even reach out to you, he can't even get to you. It's moving so fast when you're talking about a turnaround; that thing was turned around quickly, and they tried. They couldn't get to you, and they couldn't get to me. I said, "God, thank you for turning it around. Thank you for taking the reproach off of my life. Thank you, God. Thank you but lastly, be mindful of me. There's a song by Courtney Brian Wilson, and it's called "Mindful," and it says this, *"I love you because you first love me. I am thankful for your grace. I didn't know you were all I needed until you were all that I had and now all I have is you, and it's more than enough".*

The case is closed, ladies and gentlemen. God is your vindicator. He's your judge, and today and this day forward, the reproach has been removed, the courts of heaven have heard the witness, and you're free to go. Amen!

In Closing

When I was younger, New Year's Eve was a big opportunity to stay up late, eat, drink, go to a party or watch Dick Clark on television to bring in the new year. People, including myself, made resolutions which most of the time were hard to keep because the goal was unreachable. I started thinking differently about the process as years passed by and I got much older. I couldn't understand why we waited until the end of the year to figure out what to change in the next.

As I began to teach and talk to others I realized, many people don't know how to goal set. When I hired and managed people, one of the tasks would be to create 1,5- and 10-year goals. Many of them struggled and never would get pass 5 years. Why? It's too hard to think in the future about what could become. When searching for answers, the best way to stay grounded is to ask questions and research how to create a better life for yourself and family.

I am a believer, so my first task is to pray and seek God, ask my questions, get confirmation, and move forward. Sometimes I might not move as fast as I would like but I move. Every day that we are not advancing in the plan that God has for us is a sin. I have made mistakes, but God's grace is sufficient, and we need to get up and try again.

I have written this book because I want people to have a plan before the new year begins. It took Nehemiah 52 days to re-build the Temple walls of the city. It can take you the same amount of time from November 11 until December 31, in any given year; to set goals, make plans and move forward into your purpose. My prayer is that this book inspires you to think differently about your goals and your future. Let's Do This!

See you in the 11th Hour,

Dr. Michelle

Visit the website for future information regarding goal setting and future workshops on finishing strong to fulfill your destiny!

About the Author

Dr. Michelle is a Pastor, Teacher, Ambassador, and Advocate for Financial Literacy and Legacy. She is an author of many books and continues to search the Word of Truth devoting herself to continuous learning and understanding of God's plans for one's life. Her goal is to help people draw closer to Him and be an example for others of a life well lived with Jesus! Her teachings on business start-ups, financial literacy, Kingdom advancement, God's Word, and the Hebraic Calendar are just some of the revelations she passes down to this generation and the next.

Dr. Michelle has a bachelor's degree in Financial Forensics, MBA, and a Master's in Servant Leadership. Her Doctoral Studies involve understanding how mentoring women helps them to obtain leadership positions. She has devoted her time to teaching and advocating for Financial Literacy and Legacy while remaining faithful to God's Word.

To learn more about Dr. Michelle, visit:

www.drmichelledbell.com drmichelledbell@gmail.com
Facebook.com/groups/mydailybreadkingdomliving

Made in the USA
Columbia, SC
10 January 2024